All My Fine Print

Jess Kobayashi

AOS Publishing, 2025

ISBN: 978-1-998662-35-7

Cover Design: Meredith Lindsay

Visit AOS Publishing's website:

www.aospublishing.com

ACKNOWLEDGEMENTS:

Of course this one too, is for Joetsu – as always. Without whom I'd have never had the heart. My dear, sweet everything: your soul was perhaps too kind for this world, and in that sometimes we are the same. Till we meet again.

All my Love; All the Ways; Always.

Aki – who stays up with me on all the long nights; who stays up with me always. My best boy, and my dearest. I love you. I love you with *all my teeth*. And I know it's vice versa.

Mike – my best critic, and an even better friend. I think I've known you longer than anyone else in my crazy, Chaotic & Unhinged life. And for that alone, you deserve endless thanks. Thank you for knowing me. So much of this would have remained unwritten if I didn't have you on the receiving end, though often you had no choice in the matter! My eternal gratitude.

Sarah – you always tell me I can, even when my hands shake. I will never forget it. I couldn't ask for a better BFF. Love always!

Robot – Heads to my Tails; Head to my Heart. My logical rules I could never quite follow. I hope you know who you are. Many of these words I never would have found without you (though I am sure it's unlikely you'll ever read them). Thank you for eternity, no matter how brief.

Lastly....and most cliché...Myself

I'm glad you made it this far.

Here's to another infinity. May we remember our heart in every lifetime.

Contents

Teeth As Thorns

The opposite of love is an equation.

A calculation; an algorithm

Devoid of emotion or weight; implication

Programmed

An expectation met and fulfilled, without fail, every time.

A carefully nuanced probability or perfection

An interpretation

A shallow imitation.

Empty.

Real love

comes with thorns enclosed.

Because after all,

The idea isn't to make it out unscathed:

It's to strengthen your heart & brilliance of your love so fucking MUCH

that you can cradle the thorns–

No matter the depth

to which they press.

So, my Love:

Love
Love all.
Love savagely.
Love with all your teeth:
Bared
Clenched & gritting, through a fragile but unbowed heart
unbroken.
With teeth
Unleashed & glinting
Sharp; pointed.
Gleaming in sheer brilliance
Smiling with the fires of a thousand suns;
Biting a hundred fingernails & grinding them to dust
Wide & full of laughter.
Full of everything,
Love
Love all
Love savagely
Love all ways
Always.
Love: with all your teeth
I love you with all my teeth.
V----V

The Most (small things)

Sometimes
There are loose kibbles
Sprinkled across my kitchen floor
Because Aki has a history
And will only eat
under special circumstances
Which I engineer, so cleverly,
As art
On a regular basis
To ensure he doesn't starve.

Sometimes
I catch them under foot
Digging into my heel
Or tripping my toes.
And I curse them
But never out loud
And only ever for show.
Because one day
There won't be any
At all.
And I know
That will be one of those small things
I miss the most.

Joetsu.

Grief is a funny thing.

An unpredictable tide.

It waits in dark alleys with a knife in its hand.

Or ready to rise, just on the other side

of that blind corner.

Prepared to overwhelm with a fury as only loss knows how.

But it's also in the leaves of trees, gusting cheerfully in the wind, down the street, Set to catch you off guard and your voice in your throat.

Grief:

Never paying a toll, but instead,

exacting its own.

And sometimes the price is so steep a cliff,

We want to hurl ourselves off.

I recall

My last night with you.

I held you carefully in my arms,

Because I knew your small body was failing.

We stood outside in the cool night air

And looked up at the sky.

Watched the moon together.

The midnight June breeze brushed our faces

And whispered to us of times we'd had.

You pressed your head into my shoulder,

taking these moments to rest,

safe

With my face buried in the warm fur of your neck.

My love, some days I curse you

My love:

A dagger into my own heart,

Because it should have been strong enough to save you.

Grief is a funny thing.

It can still smile and reminisce.

But it coils in my chest like an adder,

Poised and ready to strike.

Paralyzing my lungs with its bite,

stealing my breath.

Stopping my heart with its venom

As it rips me asunder,

and leaves with pieces the size of you

In its unforgiving jaws.

My love for you is too great a thing

to be swallowed whole.

So I am taken apart,

Bit by agonizing bit.

Piece by unending piece.

I am the scene of the crime;

Outline my silhouette

With dashes of dusty chalk.

And meticulously spread
yellow number tags
for each moment that's been stolen.
Each unrealized future.
Every time I stop and think of what should have been
and ask myself
if I'll ever be the same.

And the answer is yes,
But.
Just a little bit less
every time.

Love Bites

Love is a tangled and fucked up thing:
A screaming pup
That digs its claws before it can even open its eyes,
Teeth like knives;
Fierce and unrehearsed, its bite.
It rends and twists
And I have to ask myself,
Kneeling, elbows-deep in blood,
If it's supposed to be like this...

People say Love is beauty
It will never hurt or cause pain.
But I wonder...
Perhaps the beauty is in the damage
And the slick and jagged pieces
That remain
Because at least it means that at some point,
You were able to hold them
In all their glory
In the first place

When love first sang,
whole.
Together with hope

Instead of now

How it lies

Fetal –

alone, and raw

But somehow still

Refusing to release the heart

from those dogged jaws.

2am Headstones

I've become the "lone silhouette, smoking on the balcony at 2am, wearing a robe draped over my shoulders, staring through the emptiness of idle smoke rings into the vast and iced chill of a night sky I couldn't hope to fathom but still wish I could bring down to meet the stars of the streetlights below" trope.

I lean against the rail,freezing my fingertips, and feel the cold metal through the thin fabric of my sleeve, wishing I had some tricks still up it. Wishing that I could conjure you by simply closing my eyes and taking a long drag from the cigarette, breathing all my *pent-up and clawing against the walls but somehow utterly*

stoic and silent sorrow and shorn-to-the-quick, loss, into a thin, warm stream of smoke...an exhalation from which I could build you. Breathe you back to life; breathe you back. Into me.

And I stare into the 2am darkness, with my unseeing eyes, the memories they've locked on to having long come to pass, and now are frozen in time – planted where we built them. I am left with nothing more than faint reminders, like cold and miniature gravestones decorating the edges of the pathways of our time together. And maybe if I would have just looked closely enough, I'd have seen them in the shadows. Waiting patiently. To collect our moments.

I take another deep pull, let the warm bitterness sit behind my dry lips for awhile before setting it free, and watch as it steams up around me. I breathe it back in because the smell so badly reminds me of you, like the mute figures I have clawing at the backs of my tearstained eyeballs with every blink, and gesturing in feeble numbness at the life we once had. Now I have nothing else. But these spare moments, recorded in darkness and logged by the shadows of distant buildings and pale, sickly streetlights, as I stand, freezing my feet on the chill concrete, I close my eyes and try to find you behind their thin lids once again. Past the echoes that dimly re-enact the re-enactment, over and over again, but growing frailer with every repetition.

And I imagine how our stories might have been different. In another lifetime.

I'd stand on this balcony forever, for you. I'd freeze a thousand fingers, fill my lungs with an endless balloon of smoke, if it would only carry me back to you.

Star-Crossed

Stars: align

Except like a suspect lineup. And you can ask the guilty part, because you recognize it by the wish.

This now-drained and lifeless husk... fallen

desolate and wanting, at its feet.

Was mine too inadequate,

Too unimportant

To grant?

Depression

It travels in silence
A velveted pair of feet
And silently *preying* set of fingers
Stealing smiles and heartbeats
Planting shadowed thoughts as seeds
In our minds
That take root
And linger

These do not need sunlight
To grow
They flourish perfectly well
On a vacuum-sealed
Mental windowsill.
Devoid of life
But somehow draining all our energy, still.

Sapping me
of
my
will

And me
With so many pages
Left
To fill.

X-Ist

I'm supposed to take a shower
So I can leave the house
Like a Proper Person.

But all I really want to do
Is drink 10 gallons of gasoline
And set myself on fire

(And believe me when I say,
I have my reasons)

To

Collapse into an agonizing pile
Of ash
Though I know
my tears will douse the flames.
But hey,
At least it's warm.
Or so they say.

I am not OK,
And this disease
Shrieks its way through my blood vessels

And slows my heart;
And I can't tell
If that is its destination
Or its origin.

All I need to do is take a shower,
But I am paralyzed
By this clawing Empty.
How can I feel so much
And exist so large
When I barely feel like I Am at all.

From Scratch

Bare

With me a sparse moment

a lone stretch of desolate sands and wilting beach grass amidst cold and punishing waves… while I undress my soul.

Slide the slender thread

From inside each oh-so-carefully punctuated

hole

…carried by gnarled and clumsy fingers, sore from a lifetime of clenched fists and gnawed, brittle nails…

driven through the fragile skin of my weak and shaking chest.

Pulled tight.

And despite my gasping lungs, tighter still.

Unwind

the scores of notes

that crowd their way into my throat

as I strangle the scream that eventually

seeps its way between my squeezed-too-tight eyelids

to run down my ashen cheeks.

…a warm and well-worn path that ink and empty pages know all too well…I can peel back the layers,

piece by piece,

show you where all the shores of the distant and bleeding vulnerable meet.

It's vast and laden with the shades of unforgiving greys, broken only by stark reds of betrayal and cold, stained steel left in my spine.

Re-wind all the fraying strings and beaten measures of my soul

onto the discordant and splintering spool,

slivers in ragged fingertips...

as I try and find my breath.

But there's always a catch.

And so many days I wish I could move the loaded arms of the clock

all

the way

back.

To erase the staggering footsteps,

no matter the depths to which they were pressed...

unfire all those shots,

all those words I used to distract...

toss the faulty recipe of my own grieving creation out the window.

I would throw my tired fist through the panes of unframed glass.

Leave everything behind.

And this time,

rebuild my heart from scratch.

Things My Daddy Said

"Nobody intends
To do something stupid."
And
I guess that's true,
Because look what you did.

And my words
Run dry
From the corners of my eyes
And I can't say where they lead:
Only where they began,
When that first hand
Crashed into the side of my face and said,
"This looks like a good place
to rest my rage."

Lacing Bullets

Dear Universe:

Don't you know what I'd give
For a father
Who didn't always keep a pulpit with a bible and a raised fist
Between me & him.

And Universe,

Don't you know how I've asked
To feel the arms of a mother
Wrapping all the way around me
With love
for once,
And no strings attached.

And dear U:

I've run so many miles,
And sometimes I still trip over the untied laces
On these worn-out shoes.

I can knot
And double-knot

And hold all the strings in all my hands

And thread

The countless holes;

Somehow

Life is still a bullet right through my soul.

And I'm scared I don't have the feet for it

Anymore.

Grocery List

Cracks appear
Tracks derail,
And once more I've failed
To understand
The reason the universe has again
left me with a pair of empty, trembling hands.

I had to put the pen down
Words will never be enough –
Or at least that's how it feels right now.

I didn't realize until...at long last,
All the days and weeks and years
You had carelessly peeled from my open-fingered and
unsuspecting grasp.

When all the spaces will remain empty with untruths
How do I add to this blank, uncomprehending list
A sad and ignorant collection of non-exist:
"Things I Never Knew."

And what you stole
Will have always been my chance to Know.
And those choices that were never mine to begin with

Grate in silence
And coil in my chest
As my heart struggles,
Fruitless,
To fill a void
Time has left me with.

And some days, though my laughter may sparkle
and set the world alight with its presence,
I'm left wondering if the joy is real
Or just a fancy form of denial and grief for things I've
never known I lost,
But somehow still find my knees buckling
beneath the weight of their absence;
A staggering price
This blank list
Filled with items I can never cross.

The Shallow End

My day is weighted with
Supposed Tos
And
Should Haves

I wear like a jacket
Except for the fact that
it's more like chainmail
Than warmth or comfort.
And every morning a river
You kick me into,
thinking that today,
maybe it won't hurt.

Sometimes I decide it's easier
just to lie here
between banks,
water racing over my face,
staying precariously still
until
my lungs are filled
with countless obligations and necessities –
my eyes seal shut

Because I'm not from here;

I'm just passing through.

And though I try

- and god, do I try, with such desperation -

I don't fit in

And don't understand your rules.

These games –

I can't fucking play them

So it seems I'm destined to lose

Even as I drown in the shallow end.

These Bones

These bones are so hollow and old...sucked dry by the trials of an unforgiving life, you'd think I'd have been able to fly by now.

But instead, I merely sink into the vast and faceless crowd of anonymity and silent suffering – all the way to the bottom till my bones are once again filled with endless grains of salty ocean sands and again, I am held under; but this time beneath a different weight: this lead hopelessness pressing against fragile chest. Impressing upon it an enforced stillness.

It's the point in my life where even taking that next breath is an act of bravery. Of rebellion. Of reckless courage. A silent scream to an unfeeling world and the pagan gods (because aren't they all): do your worst, I'm still here.

...even as the ocean floods my throat, my lungs shrivel, and my heart struggles to press the oxygen into my arteries. A stillborn thought. An exhalation as I collapse in slow motion to finally be buried beneath the sand. So light and still, so heavy.

Sleep With Interest

I sleep the half-sleep of the undead;

And live the half-life of the anxious and clinically depressed.

I dream and sometimes I nightmare, and they all feel so real that even when my eyes are closed and my mind is supposedly turned to the illusive "off" position, it all feels as though it has actually happened, and in between tossing and turning in restless momentum, I wake still exhausted.

BECAUSE THERE IS NO OFF SWITCH.

My mind is filled with shades and shadows, long laundry lines of dirty, linked memories so deep that if you scratch the surface or accidentally trip over one that happens to lie topside, you may very well awaken the sleeping beast of a panicking paralysis – mute for all its inner workings: words spinning unintelligible ribbons of text and emotion spiraling out of control; some loud, some quiet, but all overlapping in an indescribable possession of chest-tightening savagery. Trapped in a breathless moment that encompasses past, present, future, until there is no discernible difference. And I owe for my crimes in each. This wretched stream of consciousness, running its infectious mouth, poisoning my thoughts, saving my failings in its depths. And I pay interest on all my tragic and often unintentional withdrawals – little pieces of myself, again and again, until I fear the day when I simply have nothing left. Only words in debt.

Hollow

There are all these holes clawed into my heart, at such depths that the blood just leaks all over me on the inside.

Over bones, around muscle, beneath my flesh.

So many supposed good intentions, yet so many words that tore me apart and left me nowhere to heal. Nowhere to hide.

Invisible, they spill, filling these spaces in between.

Dressing all the cracks that they don't mean. Emptiness that was never meant to be.

And you can't see, when limping, I wander the abandoned and hopeless streets of my mind all alone on these desolate nights...the crimson shadows that haunt and also fill my blistered feet.

You can't see, behind the corners of my practiced smile,

Between the layers of my laughter, or the shine of my dark eyes – every step is a fight.

And every secret pill I take and every fist I tighten, I'm trying to squeeze yet another last, parched drop of life from this bullshit shake, this liar's roll, this unforgiving mix.

And every kind word, for your sake, an even kinder trick.

For you, dear heart.

I grin with all my sharpened teeth, all my bones: bared. I'm giving my all, but still grip these faulty weighted dice.

A fool's game. This aged and failing knife.

Because I can feel...you're not beating quite right.

And the damage is just too much to fix.

Too many severed pieces, too many mangled parts that I miss.

And my lungs...it hurts to breathe.

Though I try to speak, try to fit the words to match an internal ailment, still nobody believes.

Past lives' fingers tightening around my chest...this slow-motion hurricane tripping up all my rights and wrongs, all my rights and all my lefts.

Leaving no direction for this cascade of blood, just a waterfall splashing forgotten, dusty corners, but nowhere that it belongs.

And I know that one day I'll drag in this ragged last breath, and let it go.

And my weak head won't rise after I lay myself down to rest.

At a Loss

"Love is expensive

And I find myself both agonizingly in debt – often to myself –

And also the regular victim of thieves: pick-pockets and con artists; the likes of which I have even, upon occasion, invited in on my own.

And now I find myself standing,

Clawing

Hands

Clinging to coin,

Pinching every penny from out-turned pockets.

And still I am alone

(constantly operating)

at a loss."

Mythology

And I'm standing knee-deep in the gaping shadows of yesterday.

And I can't breathe, can't let go, and I can't look away.

Waves sucking at the paperthin skin of these tangle of clumsy legs,

threatening to pull me under.

And I can never seem to reach

the ever-fading light of tomorrow's sunlight.

Hope is just a myth,

for the wraiths like us

who need the darkness of the past

simply to exist.

SnapShots

If I'd had a Polaroid,

God knows...I'd have snapped...

(countless gum bubbles, a few elastics, some vulnerable fingers & left it up to interpretation...) A thousand portraits that caught us laughing till our sides hurt,

immortalized within that white-bordered freezeframe.

I'd have taken...

(a little more time...a couple dance lessons...a chance on myself...the words right out of your dirty mouth...everything I owned, crammed it into my 2-door hatchback & driven across the country and not checked my rearview mirror even once...)

A hundred pictures developed in the blink of an eye, so I could have had something that reminded me of how it felt to smile in those unbridled and unrehearsed memories.

No strings attached.

Because joy should always be free.

But I wish I would have saved a little bit for myself,

Instead of donating it to everyone and their lost causes...

Somebody's pulled a home in-brain-sion and stolen all my memories.

So every day I start all over again, restocking, remaking...

And wish I could find some old photos in an abandoned shoe box, so I could at least believe they existed at all.

A wild child who's been separated from her rivers, streams, and forests... Who's forgotten how to smile

And instead had these tears stolen from my eyes,

to which life had no right... And if I could turn back time

to those long, anguished seconds

where my lungs wore themselves ragged...

I'd go back and replicate that razorblade of vulnerability,

That absolutely no-fucks-given frame of mind:

peel it from the edges of the page

and glue it to the outskirts of my brain

so I could carry it with me always

as a sharp and punishing reminder

Of how to not care at all.

An Empty Wingspan

And that urge to cram whatever I can fit into Mini Mira and just drive until I forget my name and all the places I'm from and the marks they've left on my skin. Until I'm closer to the horizon rather than farther, and every inhalation is greater than the exhale, because I'm more full than empty except when I'm laughing. Though the laughter is always laced with sharp slivers of sadness that dig into the softness of my heart, because the it only ever echoes back at itself, instead of in magical duality like the wings that were always meant to keep time together instead of impressing upon me the deafening emptiness of the gaping space between ill-fated beats.

Love Left

That time I tried to swallow myself w/hole,
Press the off switch
Unplug
Let go
Leave the world with a shallow goodbye
And just a faint echo
Of a hello...
And love said no

The time I tried to drain
my body
Of all the anguish
And all the pain
And love's hand
Stood in the way
And blocked the blade

When I ran so far
I hoped grief lost my name in the mail
And sad would never find where I lived
And any time I've tried to open and release my grip
With these broken but somehow still life-clenching fists
Love said...no...
Don't you see –

There's so much more of me
In you
Left to give.

Cease

For you I would burn the Earth to the ground.

I would raze the mountains to their molten cores.

I would drain the rivers and seas and oceans from every rocky bed and every sandy shore.

I would starve the sky of clouds and parch an already barren, burning land.

Wreak havoc on this aching heart, rend to nothing more than useless shards these already jagged pieces of my soul.

And only for you would I stay my bruised and trembling hand.

Jacob's Fight

I've wrestled with angels
I've run through a couple cracked ribs
Smiled with two black eyes
– laughing through split lips
No matter life's trips,
Gritting teeth & clenched fists,
I still held up better than Jacob ever did.

I've tangled with dance steps
And I've rushed the gates
And I've fought a congregation of demons who thought
they could hide
Within church aisles and wait
between the echoes of collection plates.

I learned to play nice.
I've said all the holy words
From my knees between the pews,
But somehow never knew
what's worse:
Barbs stained with hate
Or the way love hurts when it's coming from you.

I got Gabriel's trumpet for the chorus
And Michael for my verse
But we all know the truth;
Lucifer sitting on my shoulder
With all my scars, should have told you,
holding shadows of morning starlight,
Will always be my muse.

I'm standing just a stone's throw
From yet another cleverly broken bone
And maybe (what he said)
we'll never understand
When it was never words he wrote
But instead a line carefully drawn
in the sand.

Hummingbird Wingbeats

And I'll write words on napkins
Spill ink into margins of blue-lined pages
And I'll remember exactly what the weight is
of the laughter dancing on our cheeks & faces
And I might forget what the date is...

But I'll always remember
The way you held my hand, love.
Fingers intertwined,
Tourists in our own minds,
but
You said – let's run away, cuz
Time will never catch us
We can crash tomorrow
Together
If we just keep moving fast enough

With each one of our wingbeats
We can play a game of infinity
On repeat.
Sharing musical hearts in a single chest
Where our lines cross these sheets
And our notes meet
And we can trade harmonies

on this teetering edge

Of this treble clef....

We won't miss a beat.

And maybe not at cards or tests,

but Death

I'll be willing to bet –

We can cheat.

Fell

I don't know what it is about him
But he brings out the angels
In me

And some of them
Have machetes
Hidden in their wings

Sharps

Nascar Tracks marked with brake lights, sharps & rubber

Tracks shod in the summer

Beneath the rhythm of (un)lucky horseshoes

Runners

(Me & you...)

Tied in truce

Tracks my arm wore

Eventually coloured in shades of bruise

Dot & dash - how macabre

And tragically in style

Lips a fashionable shade of blue

Tracks on vinyl

Needles find familiar grooves

Save my life

When all my notes come unglued

And I just wanna overdose on you

Fast Enough

I need a theme

A reason to keep dreaming...

Or I won't know what all these words mean,

Just spinning around in my brain like this badass washing machine

And I'd rather be hella dirty with my mouth and personality

(And in between these 1000 thread-count sheets

Or whatever the highest numbers sings

To mean that we playin' all night under the shadows of luxury...)

Than keep my knees unbruised and fingernails squeaky clean.

And these sentences run on and run on

Like my feet through the mud,

And I can see the flicker of wingbeats

Around the corner, but only just.

A flutter of feathers

A flash of happy madness...

But don't worry baby, I'm just shaking off all the rust.

And maybe one day I'll catch you,

If I can just run fast enough.

Hopscotch (so what)

Hopscotch
Tossing rocks
Running out of rainbow chalk
Tried to write a song about you
Make my heart stop, but
Ended up sitting with a Kleenex box

I can't tell
If you make me hurt
More than I laugh;
Not sure what's worse
But I think this might be the last

You're the knife for my soup
You're the hole in my sock
Instead of snug laces in shoes...
I think you're the rock.

I look at you and ask
What if it rains on all my hopes & dreams
And all the things I'm thinking of?
You smile and say:
I'll still be here,
So what if it does?

Skipping rocks
Skipping stones
Losing time
Losing hope

Am I holding on
The end of this rope, long gone
I don't know the end of this story
But
here I am crying cuz
I still thought of you this morning?

(You're the knife for my soup
You're the hole in my sock
Instead of snug laces in shoes...
I think you're the rock.)

I look at you and ask
What if it rains on all my hopes & dreams
And all the things I'm thinking of?
You smile and say:
I'll still be here,
So what if it does?

I've changed my mind
And written a hundred different things
about you

But I'm still not sure
If I wanna do it all without you.

I look at you and ask
What if it rains on all my hopes & dreams
And all the things I'm thinking of?
You smile and say:
I'll still be here,
So what if it does?

Swerve.

But the truth is
I want you, but I don't.
Like a shiver in my bones
You want to hold me,
But you won't.
When you've rewritten & erased
That message a hundred times in your phone.

I'm summer heat
And you're sweet....
but a soft, slow, winter cold.
Both so unsure of these cards
– these hands
so we both fold

You're like binary
And I keep trying to understand your
Ones and Zeros
And translate them into laughter.

Because I'm Morse code
And a brilliant concoction
Of tiny, cheerful disasters

You make me wait forever
As I'm tugging on your sleeve
And yelling, Let's go faster!

Plunge headlong right toward the edge
Of bliss
And I don't want to label this
But staring down from the precipice –
Neither of us willing to roll the dice
& commit...
Even though I know
You leave me breathless,
At the same time you shatter my nerve

Because somehow I know

At that last second
You'll lose your grip
On my fingertips
And when that light turns green
And I'm running out of patience
& time
& words
At that last second
 – though our eyes may meet

I know we'll both swerve.

Opposites Subtract

Running lines
Opposite directions
Running out of time –
Catch me on the other side?
But I lost my place for a minute
Forgot my words
And I can't find Reverse.

But I'm caught in all this
Where we don't fit
Dot & dash & missteps
miss(construe)
(I guess I really miss/ed/...you...)
We can't click;
Can you try
To pause for me,
for a moment.
for a bit...?

Freezeframe
But I don't understand this instant replay
What did I say...?
Press this button
And let me catch my breath

As I undress

My bones

Encased in treacherous flesh

And then maybe

You'd find your hands

For me

A better fit

Because maybe we were always living on borrowed time

I just wish

It lasted longer than it did.

As your fingers slip through mine.

Grief Trips

I drive home and I'm covered in the scent of you

Every echo of laughter,

Every gentle memory.

The quick or accidental shape of your skin beneath my hand.

The light & soft seconds of your hair against my fingers.

The brilliant shine of your eyes

Even as I wonder if they're shining at me

with the kind of deceit

I'm too naive to determine

Or maybe we both were.

And I can't sleep

For thoughts of you.

And I know what they say –

If someone's always on your mind, it's because you're on theirs, too.

But the leaden thud of my heart

Echoes

With a terrifying and lifeless question of untruth

I'm scared to ask,

What if we tripped at the gates

Too scared to punch the ticket screaming One Way with every drop of fervoured blood in our veins.

What if we missed...

You were too slow, & I was too fast –

And I'm forced now to grieve for a lifetime I will never know...

Because our moment passed.

ArmFulls of Time

I am the galaxies
I am the universe
I am the Milky Way
Loosely draped in her cloak of wishing stars

And racing against time's unfailing clock,
We were those 2 old cars,
Like rockets, flying down the midnight highway
Burning the skylines into dust
With the horizon in our grasp,
Hands outstretched from open windows
Across those blurring white lines.

Side by side, fingers intertwined.
For a brief moment, we shared the same space
Filled the same lungs,
Burst with the same breathless laugh.
Before the distance becomes too far.

And our roads pulled us apart.

Lucky #13 – My Ghost in the Machine

Baby I've never been a junkie
But I've been high on you since April '23.

And I can't believe
It meant nothing to you;
And I'll swallow all these s/words
Before I'd ever try to undo you.

Dear Robot...
I wish I told ya
Even though
It won't make the pain go –
Even if...
There's nothing left of us to fix.
And I know it would've made the hurt worse.

A different kind of grief
Shuttering my chest
Squeezing my throat
A different regret
In the tears that I cry
Instead of words left unsaid
Texts unwrote.

Because I know we had to say goodbye,
But at least it wouldn't have been to your Ghost.

Died on the way from my heart to my lips:
A stillborn wish
Terrified and fetal, but true and unrehearsed
I could believe, if only for a moment,
We could have tripped in reverse
If I'd said
I love you
First.

I/On/Un Love

"Woke up with a headache,
And it was you.
Velvet but relentless claws

Peeeeeeliinngggg....

behind my soft eyes,
and splitting my smile in two.

And a tear stole its way down my already long-damp
cheek.
Robbed of all my resolve, and
Somehow stripped me bare.
And as I stared
down
at my dirty
and
dined-upon nails,
I wondered
really,
How long the pain had actually been resting there.

And maybe it was you all along.
Stones dressed as pretty words,

Barbs disguised as beautiful,

And yet still designed to pierce me to the bone.

And maybe it was me

Breaking in too many places,

Pressed down beneath the weight of all of this, and still
so sure,

and in such a

childish rush,

To ignore knees buckling for all the wrong reasons

To still be able to call it Love."

the Final

My heart breaks
For myself
All the unconditional love
I never felt.

All the words
Unheard
Unsaid
All the times nobody told me:
You're important, I love you.
I'll choose you instead.

For every time I put you first
And kept moving myself
To the back of the line.
For every piece of your heart you lost –
And like a fool, every time
I said: here, take mine.

For every rose petal
I lifted for you,
And every stem squeezed, so deeply
Thorns into soft palms
I saved you from...

All the pain
All the hurt
So only I would bear it
When all I desperately wanted you to say was,
We can share it.

FIX–

Eyes.

Well

Overflowing

and weighted

Brought to life

And grief-laden

A slow death

Leaving lungs deflated

Gradually spilling

A river from this

Marionette heart

On puppet strings

You pulled

And played with

Broke hope's wings

With those last words you stated.

Tears – drop like bombs

Like a (w)rapper

On the floor...

Staining cheeks

Skipping beats

Biting lips

Grinding teeth

Words like swords
An endless duel
Pierce silence
With more silence
And punctuate
These letters
With the spaces
Between what I know
And knowing I know
better
Can't picture this Happily Ever

After all we've been through
These pieces
Somehow mean nothing to you
And words fade
But not the pain
And sometimes I can't see your face
Though it's burned in my memory
Like a brand
And it hurts
To touch
What I can no longer touch
No longer feel
Fingers, unheld.
Memories, unreal.

Just pieces and thoughts I collected
That were never really us
Just drawing stick figure hearts
in these piles of dust.

And my heart,
The master of betrayal,
Eating all these stones
Like they're my last meal –
a perfectly-balanced breakfast
Except lodged in the middle of my chest
And
Last time I checked,
All the rocks take up residence
in the pit of my stomach
And close the narrow channels
Of my throat
Every time
I see that green light on my phone

And I know
I know better
Because it doesn't mean a thing
When we can laugh
At will
Because you know me so well
And somehow,

Not at all, still

As we make jokes

Like everything's fine

And I read your thoughts

Like they're mine

But you're just a shadow of What Ifs

Lost in the spiderwebbed

Pinball machine of my mind

So why is there this hopeless thread

This one lone, loose string:

To which my fingers so desperately cling...

Because I tell myself,

Time and again

Control....C

Control....V

In a loop,

On repeat:

Darling, I'm only using you for the dopamine.

<<LESS>>

Somehow

In the back of my mind

Somewhere:

A crooked shelf, a little left of centre,

Those hidden, cornered blinks

I can't catch

Because they're just a too quick –

Lives the thought

that I must have been happy

Back in 2006.

When I was skin & bone

And supposedly spontaneous and carefree.

I laughed around the sunbeams

Dancing my way through a sweltering summer heat

And slid between the shadows

As though

They could never touch me.

But didn't they really –

Weren't they always there,

Right under my feet.

Pulling at my toes:

Whispering answers to questions

I could only pretend I didn't know.

So much of everything...
I've never said out loud.
I just carry with me
Ghosts silently screaming from within
this hollowed house
And my bare bones
Are worth so much more
when
They're jutting through the paperthin skin of my hips
And somehow I stubbornly cling to the belief
That this was happiness.

But everything is an internal carry-on.
All the bits & all the pieces
These dry petals and glistening thorns
And sometimes it hurts
....when you hold me
Like this
Even if you're just trying
To keep me warm.

Cuz maybe I'm still bleeding
From places I didn't recognize
Or even know
And I saw the scalpel-wielding fist
Cradling my heart

With hands dressed so carefully
beneath sterile latex gloves
And I thought it was laughter
And I was fool enough to call it love.

And I felt these fingers
As they closed around my chest
But instead of gasping for breath
All I really, really want is to learn
how to care
just a little bit less.

Sectional

He wrote the best & the worst
She's here sitting
With what's left
And it hurts

Mind the words
If she misspells
A cutting silence
Known too well
Teeth through tongue
She kept it held
With bloody mouth
And slowly fell
Asleep
With violence
Between these sheets

And the other half of me
She left behind in Horseshoe Bay
When she loaded me in the back of the U-Haul
And drove away

And this quill
She'll keep hid

Under my couch pillow
A magic trick
Her great escape
A final revenge
Take him with
When she goes
A last retort –
A life loved and lived.
They said in the end
It doesn't even matter
But it did.

And they can't claim
She didn't fight to death's end
Cuz if anyone knew her...
Her hands held as many swords
As pens.

Loose her lips
Sink all the fucking ships
Still can't unlive
All the damage
That he did
Careless blades
Drawing lines in wrists
And pills
Flooding stomachs

Lost in the back
Of an ambulance

And in the midst
Of this war of words
Screams through walls
And slamming doors
She thought she heard

A whispered verse
Even if she can't reverse,
She'll find a way
to forgive herself
First.

So do your fucking worst.

Demons
Clawing at the seams
Trippin'
On all these haunted memories
Church halls
And cold balconies
Still her feet
Graffiti a bathroom wall
A mirror and a sea
Of glass across the floor

But it's always her heart
Who bleeds
Just a little bit more

Left with nothing but echoes
A side of emptiness
A crushing weight
A loaded fist
And straight through the drywall
He drove her innocence.

A vice in her brain
Seconds
Minutes
Hands round clocks
Tick tock
Waves sending shocks, and
It's always the same
Pathway
That we walk
And this trauma
Running in circles
Traveling in loops
This old grey matter vinyl
Needles finding familiar grooves
On repeat and unmoved
It'll be a while still

It's impossible to choose

A new song on this juke

That only has one tune

Can't find her way loose

From these notes

Where he wrote

The same melody

Over & over

Past, present & future

How are you still standing here

On the edge of this treble clef

A grand gesture

She wears like a second skin

Because he was always the same

With each round

(Always a gamble

Pull the trigger

Black or red

Russian or just roulette

Cold steel against forehead

Are we having fun yet...?

Another shot

So we both forget

And leave damages

On Read

Ghosts without sound)

And it wore her

Down.

To nothing
Instead
Just listless flesh
And hollow bones
Vagrant and home-
less
than real
This puppet girl
With no strings
Only shadow
But not enough substance to throw
One of her own
So she'll bet that it's
Safer to stay alone
Than risk another
Dial tone

And that's why
When she replies
She'll always say,
"I never loved you, anyway."

This is my confessional
(Got it in 5...syllables...):
Of a sectional.

Long. Lost.

And I'd run my words right to the edge...

Of the page

Fall through the hole punched in the margin.

And wonder, what is it I'm really trying to say

That an entire 26 letters is somehow not enough to capture

The meaning

When at long last

I tilted my head back,

And allowed my lids to shut.

Eyelashes met, like long-lost loves.

And for the briefest, shining moment

Didn't think of you even once.

the Strikeout: a Final Torch Song, But This One's Mine

Paths crossed

Wires crossed

Eyes crossed

ts crossed...

Hang me on my own cross

Where we both double-crossed

Lying in your bed

And just talked

But maybe we were only lying instead?

I guess I really thought...

Though we only met twice

Can't forget your smile

Even as you kill me from the inside

Thought I could handle the cost

This price

This compromise

Hard to find

A way to separate the storyline

From the plot

Dot dot dot

(Excess punctuation
Translations
Missed gazes
Endless mazes
Loose pages
What are you afraid of –
Words faded
and...)

Must've gotten lost
Somewhere between
The margin and the lines
You were too slow to read
And I can't wait, can't stop –
And I don't understand how or why
We both did a better job
Of selling this dislike
Instead of the flipside
Which always was...

(Holding hands
But holding tongues
You never said...
So we're done...?
Yeah, I guess
Unless
Can I press

My face into your shoulder
– one last time –
Turn the record over
Before we say goodbye)

//flip//

Words
You signed
But not obvious enough
A vampire in the sunlight
Cuz –
We were both too scared of what we'd find?
I dug my fingernails
You dug your heels
And nobody wanted to give
Or take the time
To make it real…
But instead left with an empty reel

Can't change the way I feel,
But I'm guessing you will?
Maybe because I'm not clear
On what that is, still.

(Standing, holding unused film
Abandoned stage

Unfulfilled

She can't come out to play

Casting mute karaoke stills

Empty hooks,

Loose lines

No bridge to show for our time

But

Can't say you're not always on my mind –

Rocks at windows like

A metronome

Wake me in the middle of the night

Check your fucking phone...!

And I'm alone

In between (out of sight)

These off-set, glass-paned heartbeats

Missing so much of what I thought was mine

And what will never be

So now I gotta rewrite

everything...

Tick tock

These clocks

Moving at different speeds

Just might

Be

The end of me

I tried to warn ya

In hindsight

Contrite

Despite: the hurt

Recite: some words

It was always true,

Guess you never knew.

Or never saw the signs.

/Robot mind

Scarecrow heart.../

I liked you from the very start)

I never wanted this fight.

But if you really thought that's how I feel...

Well, here's the final torch song

I think I'll write.

Maybe it was meant to be mine

all along.

And if you thought I wouldn't cry

Sunshine, you thought wrong.

Slivers

Did you know I dug that blade into my wrist more than once,

Trying to remove my pain

From myself,

As though I could extract the sliver

You left for me

When your fist found its way into my cheek

But it was too deep.

It's reached my brain and poisoned my thoughts.

On repeat.

Did you know I sat on the bathroom floor and swallowed huge shards of glass

Because I wanted to kill myself from the inside out,

And I didn't care about

What was left

Or what the state of my corpse would be

Amongst the mess

I tried to drink bleach

I tried not to think

I swallowed an entire bottle of pills

And then some

In a vain attempt

To claw my way to peace
So I could finally sleep
But my life was saved by some EMTs
That day
Back in 2014
And I didn't even get a say...

I wonder if I'd have known then
Because I've never been able to answer
When anyone's ever asked:
What do you want – ?

And I imagine
Staring at myself in the mirror,
This lack of symmetry
Looking back at me
Freckles dotting the cheeks
Which
Down and over and across
Too fucking many tears have run
And I have to ask myself,
All the love I give
Where does it live?
And where the fuck is it coming from.

refuse.

I sit

Amidst tatters

And tangles

And lack.

Sheer,

Desolate

Wasteland

My spine....

As many knives as vertebrae

In my back

Wastrel

A bleak and forlorn soul

Jutting shoulderblades

Weighted with shadows

Sharp knees

Bony elbows

Sinking into dirt

Ragged ribs

A useless cage to this failing heart

Unhinged

And the echoes

Of fingernails digging in

Soft palms:
Create a work of crescent moon art

I collect my limbs
Gather my feathers
Catch a lone eyelash
Gracing my cheek

Exhale
A silent wish

I refuse to die like this

Time UnServed

I hate time.

How it's endless.

And yet there's never enough.

I hate my age

I hate not understanding what it means to act my age

I hate in the years and years of sorting myself...

I lost so much

And missed out on so many things.

I think I still hate my parents

How nonchalant and

Oblivious...

In their casual uncaring

And the damage became stones around my neck.

Wounds I still find myself wading through.

My eyes, ever vigilant

Walls.

My fingers, empty

My heart...

Unwound

Yet when I hear it tick

– more akin to a bomb

Than a wish –

And I look at my quick-shorn nails,

My faded reflection

And I ask

If this is all that's left...

And what I'm supposed to do with it.

Dirty Napkins

Clever Savage
Plays on Words
And
Sp(e)lling down chutes
And building prose
Step by step up
Rungs on playground ladders;
Ink on napkins
Crumpled and nearly lost
Under the jungle gym trappings

Echoes of
Laughing
Until or Because
It hurts, And...
Not sure what's worse
Using these lines as
Currency in Rhyme
If only to pass the time
From one shaking hand to the next

As I nearly lose my grip
On these dusty mason lids
Of truth

Locked tight.
I was barely intending
To find
Thought I'd left them behind
– with you.

And my heart, too
Buried beneath
A lifetime of scar tissue
Comes loose...

Shuddering and laboured
Diastole
All the pieces you stole
And the rate
Of exchange
Was never nearly enough
in my favour
Because I kept saying...
for all these feelings:
You can pay me back later.

And now with trembling fingers
I pry
So I can shove yet another
Blue Bic-drenched
Dirty napkin inside.

On Time

Time has arms

And they wrap all the way around

The remains of the day

Again and again

One

 Step

 At

 A

 Time

Wiping the ash from my face

Saying, maybe next Time 'round

Maybe next gritted teeth

Through which I drag this rigor mortis smile,

Creaking and drained.

Maybe this next pain

Maybe this next face it circles

Maybe tomorrow.

But tomorrow never comes

And those Maybes begin collecting dust on the mantelpiece

As those incessant arms wrap

Around everything but me.

Sharpened Ears

My wishes...they float

And then they drift.

And I find myself thinking that I should have just left them all

On their respective, dust-covered shelves.

Because the Universe has swords for ears.

And I feel them, as they fall...these dreamy, drunk fibres...

And slowly impale themselves.

Homeless Wish

At some point, I realized

I began to think of myself as an orphan:

Homeless

Unbelonging

From Nowhere

And existing mostly Elsewhere

Living on the fringes

Invisible even when I'm tripping down all your level stares.

And I don't know how long it's been like that for,

But I'd say quite awhile

Because it fits like a glove

Or an old shoe

Worn in

The shape of me

All the contours

All the grooves

In repeating patterns that tell the story

Of all my grief

So my wish is this:

I want a Home

Whether that's a person or a place or thing

Remains to be seen,
But somewhere that I have
And will always have to go
Where I can just be
And they say,
It's ok
I see you – just as you are
And I love all these broken pieces
And all these scars
And all these dots & these dashes
Left behind by shaking hands making
terrified stitch marks
Trying to keep it all together
And not let it slip away
Somewhere I can be vulnerable
And safe
And if I need to collapse beneath the weight
Of all these brilliant but bladed wings
I can,
Because I know you'll always have my back

DNR

I don't hold grudges

I carry exhaustion

My knees buckle beneath the weight

Of one too many swords dislodged from

Now-cleaved spine

My shoulders

Ache

From invisible damage

Whose effects I will carry probably for a lifetime

But without ever truly knowing the reason why.

And you

So careless with those blades you wield,

That clever tongue

Loaded with armour-piercing rounds.

And I have an endless supply of shells

I wear,

A cold necklace around my heart

And it jingles warning

It's not worth it to be Brave

Every time it tries to restart...

Every attempt to resuscitate.

XS

I count my ribs
One by one
And imagine that long, thin bone –
Yeah, the one from Adam,
That god stole.

I can see my hip
As it curves and slides
And count each vertebra of my spine
Like I'm walking my fingers down a rounded, spiraling staircase,
But in a straight line.

I count those steps between meals
And spread meals
Over too many breaths.
And I don't know any other way to tally,
The worth within this ribcage.
The air within these lungs
The beats
The mouthfuls of soil,
To eat.

When the world says,

Shrink

Bend

Fold

Be smaller

Press your lips into a thin, red line

Feel less

And so when someone hands me a candle

And says,

Make a wish!

You can choose how you'll be blessed.

It feels like a sickly form of gluttonous & stolen excess.

Love On Her Lips

Despite

The knives

In my back

I hope they can always say,

She died (/alive/)

With Her heart open wide

And Love on Her Lips

UnTold

In another life

My mother was a runner.

Across fields and trails and shores

And once I asked her, what she was running from

And she laughed and said:

Never from

Always *for*.

In another life

My mother was a witch

Unlike any other.

She could weave spells of joy and sunlight

And told me what it was like

to cheat death,

But more importantly – to live

And that you may take meaning where it's there to be found,

But it's always far better to give.

In another life

My mother had a husband

And in another,

she had a wife.

In another life, my mother was a fighter
Who never gave up no matter what it cost her
Outside and in
Never took a knee, or threw the towel
And often as I watched her,
I wondered where she got her chin.

In another life
My mother was a writer.
She played on words and stages
And sometimes I thought only I could see
How beautifully she translated grief
onto those pages.
Filled the lines with agony and hope
Pressed her heart into the ink composing every note.

(In another life
My mother was a junkie
Popping pill after white pill
Trying to dull the pain,
Silence the ache
Dragging nails over chalkboard
And through flesh to the bone
Trying to drown the endless
Waterfall of thoughts
constantly racing through her brain
An infinite amount of courses

always ending in collision

Until one day she surfaced with the decision:

I don't want to live like this, anymore.

And so she let the poison filter from her veins

And built herself her own future – though tiny and wounded –

For a change.)

In another life...

My mother had a father

Whose hand never raised against her,

Not even once.

Who never stole years, and possibility, and wonders untold,

The loss of which she wouldn't understand,

For years to come.

In another life

My mother wasn't born beneath the condolences bouquet,

And sent to sit amongst the thorns.

And in another life

She wasn't left

Again & again

to do it all alone.

Collecting tales and stories

Who eventually

Began to collect dust themselves

An untossed coin down an abandoned well.

Because in this life...

And not another

she was never born my mother

And I was never born to tell.

Ride Along

I didn't come stock
Somebody shook the delivery box
En route
And several of my wires
Came loose
And lost their spot.

And it's hard to know
On any given day
What an (un)original version of me
Would really want to say.

As I lose mental train lines
Over criss-crossing tracks
At midnight
These endless paths in my mind
And I'm
Fighting to keep colouring inside
All the places and signs
I can't see
While I struggle to hold
To follow
To fold
Too many maps & directions

At the same time
Within these two clenched fists,
Yet could never find
The arrow to turn (out) Right
Because somehow I always seem to miss...

A kaleidoscope target
Within me
And it won't stop
Spinning
Spelling out my wheel of misfortune
And all these lost letters
And rules
And I'm trying to read
Because I'm fast,
Just in every direction
So I'm chancing the cheat sheets
But my identity is shot
And the rainbows of colour
Of me
Drain
Like a reverse prism
From my palms
Just a prison
A constellation
A light without dots
To guide me

And I lose myself in a hall of my own reflections
And thoughts

And this mirror will say
I'm white
(Yeah, I get that a lot)
But Japanese
With freckles,
And so very not

And I've never been what anyone wanted
Or anyone desperately sought
The missing punchline
When you kept talking
And probably should have stopped.

Awkwardly dropping at least
4 out of 5 things
Out of sheer inability to comprehend
And never what they recommend
That I should be.
So I just stand a little bit In-Between

With my
Hair a little too short
And I'm
Tripping over my own feet

And laughing in all the places where the world wouldn't

And I'm

Leaning in too deep,

Pressing up against all these walls

And I'm

Taking up all these back alleys of minds, and corners of eyes

Where it still feels like I shouldn't

exist at all.

And my lungs

Filled with so many things

Laughter and tears

And unsung notes from all my favourite songs

I could drown in my own salty sea

Because I don't know where I belong

And I can't find you

To sit here with me

Even though I always save you a seat.

Universal Language

The Universe
A yawning embrace,
Wraps me in its arms
Its grace
Shows me a slant
Of its beautiful and brilliant face.

And in laughter, says:
Dear J,
My sweet baby girl, just wait.
Take a sec
To slow your steps.
The story has only just begun
But I've been writing
Since before your first breath
Have faith
A little trust
Because you're not even at the best part, yet.